Crowd Sensations

for NBB

Crowd Sensations

Judy Brown

Seren is the book imprint of
Poetry Wales Press Ltd.
57 Nolton Street, Bridgend, Wales, CF31 3AE
www.serenbooks.com
facebook.com/SerenBooks
twitter@SerenBooks

The right of Judy Brown to be identified as
the author of this work has been asserted in accordance
with the Copyright, Designs and Patents Act, 1988.

© Judy Brown 2016

ISBN: 978-1-78172-315-9
ebook: 978-1-78172-316-6
Kindle: 978-1-78172-317-3

A CIP record for this title is available from the British Library.

The publisher acknowledges the financial assistance of the Welsh Books Council.

Cover Artwork:
Sam Smith, Untitled Pour Painting no. 15, 2015.
courtesy the artist and Project Art Works.

Author Website: www.judy-brown.co.uk

Supported using public funding by
ARTS COUNCIL
ENGLAND
LOTTERY FUNDED

Contents

Crowd Symbols: Fire. The Sea. Rain. Rivers. Forest.
Corn. Wind. Sand. The Heap. Stone Heaps. Treasure.
— Elias Canetti, chapter heading from *Crowds and Power*

... the effort needed in order to see the edges of
objects as they really look stirred a dim fear ...
— Marion Milner, *On Not Being Able to Paint*

After the Discovery of Linear Perspective

You gave us new places to hide. Arcades and piazzas are excavated
from your backgrounds in diptychs and altarpieces, just for the hell.
Some of our local heroes turn out to be smallish men. They whisper

to their spotted hounds whilst the eaves of their homes recede. Stairs
strut and coil like tempters behind the colour-coded Holy Family,
the bishops, the patrons, the endlessly-bystanding centurion. We all

toe the lines, the vanishing points, the black-and-white ostentation
of floors. Perhaps the molten paint matters more than what's painted:
this has become one of your tools, a closeted flourish of show and tell.

Yet I miss their warmth: the maidens and saints twisted to press
at the picture plane, all breathy frottage, and damp like flowers under glass.
Come, technician, let us brush past the samey glamours of Joseph

and Mary. Christ, there is so much gorgeous air explaining itself
in the back of your painting! Let's inhale its new space, shout
merely to gather echoes, make gestures that astonish us.

The Astronauts

Hey, we missed the whole thing.
     – Buzz Aldrin to Neil Armstrong after watching
         videotapes of press coverage of the moon landing

Each one of us was a firstborn. It was winter
then, cut-glass solstice daylight. The stars
were just holes in some sky. The baby's room
was the study re-emulsioned in pastels,
its ceiling hung with the low fruit of mobiles.

We were the first to come close to the moon.
Family was learning to read the horoscope
of your worries: Herod's fingerpaint never far
from the door-jamb. We came to want to tip out
into thin air, to follow no one, crouch in capsules.

But the real action was back in the living room:
you, poised in your Dralon recliners; the show:
our stumbles in big shoes. So it came to pass.
The nursery light left on over the blue planet,
we fell home, boxed and bouncing in titanium,
re-entry just a sizzle in the Gulf of Mexico.

This Is Not a Garden

This garden, in fact, may not even be entered.
    – from *A Guide to the Gardens of Kyoto*
        by E. Marc Treib and Ron Herman

This is not a yard, this is a garden:
new decking slatted over a tumble of roaches.
This is a yard full of potted tropical flora,
the lotus swimming in its own pool,
mosquito-eating fish guarding its stem.

I can't know whether this is a yard
or a garden, though we ate out here last night,
the iPod snicking in its dock, soft lighting
making silhouettes behind the trellis.
This is not a garden, this outdoor, hosable sofa

or this bed where we never both sleep well.
It is a sort of park, public in places, this marriage
where amusements are scheduled and planned.
This garden, this marriage, is divided into rooms.
In some, others are welcome, like yourself.

This yard, this marriage, this bed, should be
like a garden – so many topics victim
to the secateurs. It should pass like a wave
through the seasons, appearing to be young
or else gnarled, wholly taken by age.

A man made this garden for me, whether
I liked it or not. After I had gone, he let it
go wild, to armoured holly and hawthorn,
the small beer of thugweeds, but in time
it will settle, a wiry daisy meadow, well-fenced.

A Trapped Rat Finds Another Kind of Freedom

Weeks ago Darren folded his latex gloves and sealed
his icebox of poisons; and you have nibbled
the pink sachets of pearlescent freshbait (enough
to bump off a trio of rat mafiosi). You scattered
the empties − deflated as half-dissolved balls of bath gel −
along with your coffee-bean spoor, under the stairs.

When I come back there's just you and me.
I can smell your death the moment I unlock the door:
cool and troubling in the air's petrolish by-blow;
then I see you, pretending sleep on the sofa (O, Jesus,
the sofa), utterly visible, claws clutching the flex and plug
from the lamp. Perhaps you've started to mummify −

a nice touch with the designer toxins I paid for, to save
my queasy stomach at having you snuffed. The little I do
is acknowledge your body, inhale the bitter message
of your endgame, of glacier and permafrost, roll you
off the sofa blanket, knot you into black plastic's
comfort: do the basic things one does for the dead.

The Unbeliever Speaks to God

It's not what you think: I really would
knuckle down for some mnemonic
mirrorball god. *Test me*, I'd say. I'd sew
my cringing skin with your thousand names
in every numbered shade of embroidery silk.
I'd walk away, shedding my life's collections,

slide my rings into the storm drain. I'd take
to the fleshless life — *test me* — among the dunes.
I'd be a holy fool — one of those bird-legged
ones, cinnamon-eyed — who dip and bend
to the salty trash, and once in a while raise
some floated trinket into huge oceanic light.

Test me, then — with temples slung with glitz.
I'd gift my fandom to the first bogus comer,
snared by bling and smoked-glass veneer.
Of course I'd fail: dole out burnt offerings,
glyphs of pickled ginger or flown-in mangoes,
libations as old as dust and with lees as dry.

I've often wondered what those bone-thin
gurus gave up: you went one better.
Test me, you said. As good as your word
you watched your son, lame in his borrowed skin,
be chased to the cross, mud on his hands and face.
It's as I guessed. You don't deserve me yet.

The Street of the Dried Seafood Shops, Sheung Wan, Hong Kong

Whole seas had their brine boiled off
to fill this sweating mile with desiccated stuff.

Here are plastic cartons of merchandise:
all this tissue scraped from life's float, and dried

to filigree; the ruinous bisque of dog-chew, spoils
of dirty hand-to-hand wars, where, victorious,

you fondle some enemy's sun-baked leather
cuddled into a spirit familiar to tell luck and weather.

I stumble past the fronds of calamari, frozen
mid-Mexican wave, eye cockled sheets of pemmican.

Trams spark and rattle under their tense electrics
dusting the piled kilos of brown mussels, complex

as rucksacks with their laces and straps. I gulp
air at the mereness of nuts and pulses,

shift to guilt at my desire to possess one bent
relic: this ribbed skate-wing beached on the pavement.

I kept walking because I could make no sense of it.
After a mile or so, I tell you, I was dry as a drill bit.

I dock at the Irish pub awash with happy hour,
one more beery dog-fish in a bled-out harbour.

The Dehumidifier

The air grows wetter by the hour: my breath
adds to the exhale of the soil-banked wall.
While I'm gone you'll suck it dry. Your humming
motor drives the downing of a hundred pints.
Night and day, inhuman lungfuls pass across
your plastic gills. How the rest works I can't tell.

Perhaps you harm the air so much it cedes
its dampish gift without a fight. I'd prefer
that somewhere in your workings bracken uncrinkles
and, above, on cool-touch branches, wetness gathers
like a troupe of sea-monkeys taking their rest.
A seeker might find peace inside your frost-caves
as moisture ripens and falls into the pooling jug.

By Friday it's the usual story: your green light bleats
red: you've drunk your fill. I click out the reservoir
and pour away the absent week's wet harvest,
wasting what you worked so hard to build.
Once more I will myself to neither cry nor sweat:
hereafter I may live as aridly as decency permits.

Just About Now

Just about now they are stopping my father's heart.
Of late the aortic valve has grown sluggish but all
in all, it's a fine machine, a liquid-full system,

intolerant of blowback, logjam and tides. It's been
running eight decades, systole-diastoling the miles
with its engineered bass-note. Now they are cooling

his body to reduce its oxygen-thirst while they work.
At university he studied the moody strength of materials.
He knows there are reasons why moving objects might

start to fail. On his lecturer's notes he read, upside down:
Argument weak: speak loud. Last night, at the hospital
no one changed their tone by a decibel. They've told him

a heart like that, big and hidden, rumbling in its housing,
will re-start itself afterwards, with a twitch. That's how it was
with him: downing the tea at the service station, swiping

the last of the eggs with the Little Chef toast. Time
to get on, the motorway sliding, as empty as it used to be,
between the heathered shoulders of the fells.

The Imposters

You are no sister to the flat-pack bookcase
conjured from slabs of beechfoil, and sawdust
soaked in fish-glue. Don't fall for
his surface talk about the seasons: the wet rise
of sap in spring, thin pickings of winter sun.

He's shifty as a Renaissance eye-trick fresco,
just plastic printed with treen. He'll tell you
you may trust to MDF: steadier than today's
light-minded timber, which grows soft-hearted
in a few short seasons and warps at any weather.

I'd say: don't settle to write your life story
at some burlesque plank, eschewing elm, ash
and deal. Don't take actors for your brothers,
faces made up with scars which a tree earns
from drought, flood, lightning's crash and burn.

Old wood is slow to rouse and slow to state
its bent anger, slower still to mend when lopped.
Run your hand along a Victorian windowsill,
bare-grey under its flayed paint, and still sound.
Dream of whiskey in tanks of Oregon pine.

Keep slices of the true stuff to hand, to eat off,
to clog to the shed for coal, to cradle babies,
books. Sit alone and orphaned by the blaze
of an oak's cremation, wood-coloured drinks set
on a table. Come close as family at a funeral.

The Dive: Town End, January 2013

William had slept badly—it snowed in the night
        – Dorothy Wordsworth, *Grasmere Journal*, 6th February 1802

—a most frightful Dream of a Woman whose features were blended with
darkness catching hold[ing] of my right eye & attempting to pull it out
        – Coleridge, *Notebook 849*, 1800

I could hardly move in the mornings
in those first iced-out months, spoken for
by the hollowfibre freight of two duvets.

It was drift and stream, some skull theatre
played out in cold and necessary moves,
where the Devil lounged at my shoulder –

not touching but the stretch of his side
blazed behind me, the numb happiness
that beguiles hypothermia. When he left

I lay hours in a fisherman's silence, listening
for some catch in the air. Or cramped
at snow whispers from cars on the A591,

unable to grip sleep until the boiler's strum
swam through the radiators at six a.m.
I wasn't the only one trolled by horrors

at nightfall, but the silver joy of insomnia
scared me more: the immobility I was held to
all winter, afraid to check the dials, afraid

to see that I'd been down too long.
I broke surface to bruises, a slovenly thaw.
Spring was birdsong loud as broken glass.

Skymap Says We're Nowhere Near Home

In Economy's cramped haul it's all I ever watch.
Our course is laid on screen before me, a dotted line
miles wide, plotting the next ten dry-eyed hours.

This kind of travel is the loneliest of procedures:
solo-piloting a pale track above computer-graphic
continents. Across the aisle a blindfold man dreams,

ears cupped to rattling Springsteen. It's for me
that the names of India's cities ride at the horizon,
that a picture aeroplane hauls its cartoon shadow.

As I glaze over, the tracking shot pulls back:
the round planet is ribboned with aerial desire paths.
Our destination blinks and spins like a mandala.

Nine hours, eight minutes. Below us, Japan:
its wounded power station close to cracking open.
On someone else's jumpy screen, grim Clint chews

a cigar. I'm held by my haloed book, unwrap
a tray-arrayed banquet. Friday the thirteenth:
pray for us, seat-struck, each in our private light.

Poem in Which I Am Not Shortsighted

First: surely myopia is a priestly calling,
where the world falls short in long isinglass halls.
Here souls flit like floaters, intransigent,
and the clear image crystallises forward
of the retina, oracular as a twist in a marble.

Secondly: resolution will never come to pass.
Even the finest lasers freeze at this degree
of negativity. It's easier to see myself eyeless,
orbits cored and caved. But I am tempted:
I imagine such a poem, and I want in.

Thirdly: short sighting's a matter of too much,
the whole 3-D backstory, the eye so stretched
it's water-sculpted as a barrel jellyfish.
At 20:20 it would all be different: my eyes
round as real globes, doll-painted, factory-fresh.

I admit that I once woke on a coach without lenses,
and at four a.m. could read the green LED
of the driver's clock. It was a temporary cure,
but it was fine: the ripping away of cloth;
miracle, with its tinsellish, lottery-win tocsin.

Where to Begin a New Life

Perhaps at this border, where my skin's seal
nudges the wet air and where mosquitoes
patrol, nipping and puckered up to get in.

Fifteen years ago my legs flowered
into blisters of body-filtered water. Now
my connective tissue flows slowly back

through time until I understand where
I am. The place knew: I was a returner,
had borrowed some of its diesel-perfumed air

for my own signature blurt of pheromones,
eaten yard-long beans grown from a feed
of night-soil, had drunk imported wine,

cool and costed as the nights started to thin.
It's coming back: how I started where
you're starting now, in an empty flat, glass-

floored with new varnish. I know how the sun
comes misty-sly over the painted hills. By
eleven I'd beg for fog at the curtainless blaze.

The thermostats are set to absolute zero;
we still shed moisture. Just watch it rise
into a sweat of saltwater pearls on our chests.

The Prodigal

Am I kidding myself that you hauled me back
to this bucket of hills? Your kind of paradise:
a bright green cloth pressed over my face. I'm gagging
to box up my books, give the slip to your screes.

The air's not right, a fairy food which spoils me
for the honest flavours of smog. I'm hungry,
gnawing at slabs of your prickly gingerbread.
If I stayed, would you call off those dreams?

These fells want the lot. I'm stranded in half-dark,
while they vamp on the tops, admiring themselves!
In the valley our conversations run on a loop;
monomanias ricochet and return off the slopes.

Say I recant? You'd shut the pass, and pen me
in your slate-studded hold. That's what I ran from
years ago, lungs gulping for some future I saw.
Behind me your magnetic field hardens to storm.

The Third Umpire

always was, his noonday elder brothers said,
the piker in the pavilion, pale as milk.
Raspberry feathers ring his albino irises.
He soaks up the behind-blind daytime dark,
dreaming before his bank of shut screens.

They'll call on him soon, the two sun-faced
umpires, to liven and lean in to his images:
master of instrument and replay. Then
his muscles will tense to some sunk mood.
It's his cold call, what happened to that cloudy hit.

He's the dead boy whistled into the table-glass
to speak true. And will — where the stitched ball
left a kiss on the glove shows as snow on Hotspot.
The played bat always bled unboiled linseed
from its wood, but no snick of sound is heard here.

This is new to him, being set over his brothers
and Hawkeye, haruspex, tells him what might
have been but for the intervener, plays the delivery
in dotted lines as if the batsman was just air,
where it would have gone if it hadn't gone awry.

Some nights he walks bare-chested onto the pitch
and touches the square for some last warmth.
His skin itches under an owly moon.
He can hardly believe it: that the crease belongs
to the umpire, and thus can be said to be partly his.

He lays his talc-dry thumb in its chalked dent,
knowing the real miracle is that the game flows
out here, the click-fizz of shook beer blossoming.
If his brothers had him thrown onto this grass furnace
at noon, would his god really let him burn?

A Preparation for Loneliness

Start by recalling that girl's howl, thirty years back,
at her hand trapped (and worse than trapped)

in a thrown-shut train door at Fenchurch Street.
Read around the subject: how a man on holiday

ran through the sun-crisped maquis, right off a cliff.
He was cylindered home in the coolbox hold

of a scheduled flight. Keep going back to them:
to people chosen to play themselves, at the front

of a crowd scene of the hale and hearty: the one
picked from his peers by the sniper, eyes valving

to holes, turns to flee. Or someone is rendered –
the straightjacket flight, suppository-drugged

and waterboarding to come. The wind rushes in.
It's early days. No scholar, you can't yet imagine

even the quieter tragedies: to sit on cardboard
outside Tesco Metro, never as drunk as you want,

face as bright as a rufous fruit. Even less,
how to stand at a blown-out window, aflame.

Umami

With ginger tea, with steak on blue porcelain,
her husband's cooking plays my spicy tongue,
riffs on its various areas: salt, sweet, umami.
He chivvies us into sourness like a personal trainer –
serves Japanese since her doctor forbade chilli.

It is ginger we keep coming back to: the tingling
rhizome. Its pageant flowers drip in every vase
in their house. I brought ginger nuts from England.
She wanted hard biscuits against the chemo's nausea,
the kind she once crunched on cross-Channel ferries.

The terrace swarms with plants which none of us
were born to. The strength goes out of our bodies
in the conditioned air. Ceiling fans swallow
time – supercool and slow – but nothing
can stop the humidity from softening the biscuits.

While I play tourist, her fast cells are decelerated
by what the nurse infuses into her bruised vein.
These are the last-discovered things: umami, Pluto,
the masked facts of the way things are. We eat
meals alive with fish sauce. None of this is exotic.

Long Range Forecast

In deep old age I plan to potter in a garden flat
just down the road, to stumble from room to room;

or outside, patting the swollen trees, survivors of pollard
and amputation — grown cactus-squat and cautious.

My ankles will be the same: fat and pillowy, bone's
true story hidden beneath the soft anecdotage of fluid,

a long time telling. People write books so quickly now.
From mid-life on, I'll be ready with tissues and paracetamol —

small cures for the long haul. Menthol to chill the pulse-
points. Ginger for sickness at sea, and on land.

The Things She Burned That Year

Whole nights claimed her on sooty knees,
worshipping the heat of a first open fire.
She tended it with the caution of a mistress,

offered her past and part of her future.
She kindled her half-filled diary; each curling
page exposed the inky, unburned next.

All afternoon it read itself to the blaze,
settled down at dusk to a soft grey bed.
She was watching someone she knew grow old.

Then she'd fed the fire a banquet of porn
that she no longer had an attic to store.
The printed bodies, the breasts and cocks

were nibbled off by a bright green flame
before the paper charred in the usual way.
And the final text that lanterned out

in the beige-tiled fireplace flared so fast
that the thing she wanted to erase
was lost: even its capsicum name is dust.

The Green Man

... the mouth is indeed a strait place, the prototype of all prisons.
                                        — Elias Canetti

The locals stand at a distance, then approach;
their stares scrawl in nettle-sting on his skin.
No sign explains how to pay, or for what.

Silence rolls in his and their mouths, a pebble
that quenches every thirst but his. He carries
no confession he could exchange for forgiveness,

is offered no last shave, favourite meal, a dram.
In the fisticuff alleys, all he knows is secession.
He twitches in rooms, that until he entered

were full of arm wrestling and long bonhomie.
Nothing said can be overheard in his presence.
He knows them only as a householder learns,

too late, of the hornets whose ghost nest
is slung from the barge boards, is told nothing
of their rustling cities on whose outskirts he drifts,

or what badge he had worn at the frontier
that other men turned away to speak instead
to women, which led him to take to the hills.

Up there, no one else claimed the bedroll
of fog that lay in the valley, or moved back
or forward, to hinder him, or to let him pass.

Songs from West Cumbria (1)

The Corner House B&B

Carlisle does not welcome me as the rain welcomes me,
skiting my rucksack with buckshot hail
as I walk up and down London Road's skewed map.

It's a good room when I find it: clean and smelling
of the last traveller's Ralgex, two huge Velux windows
peeling off the roof to the white-bread sky.

The neighbours' dogs are full of luck, and snarling.
Shed your last crisp youth, suffer under the all-night
deafen of slammed car doors, and ten yards down

outside the pub, they're sipping to the year's first
warm night: men hooting like elephant seals, their girls'
half-serious harmonies tuning themselves to glass.

Unsafe Harbour

I can't know what she knew when she found it
in her breast. I'd second-guess: a node
whose meaning had mustered a crowd.
Her fingers read: a clan of bad facts;
a sea yarn that might tip, at some low hour,
and turn tricoteuse, knotting to tumour.

She hoped it would keep to its own kingdom,
an isolate city with sealed gates. Gossip says
the danger lies in the ports, where trade routes
tangle and freed news turns feral. Here sailors
scatter their king's shillings. Flotsam coiling
in the lymph's afternoon tide catches here.

Neck, armpit, and groin – these are places
of grain and pulse – basin and channel where
ships pause to spill their cargoes, where hawsers
tear into their moorings. Here knowledge
is unloaded; things start to heat. When the surgeon
cut it loose, it had this story to share.

Songs from West Cumbria (2)

The Leaks: The Golf Hotel, Silloth

I was going to tell you I loved squally Silloth
even before the man in the Kandy Store defended it
saying it was a good place but for the year's rain.
The pavement seafront invited me to step down
the amphitheatre steps into a slurry-brown sea.

My love deepened as I watched the sun dip
behind slanted pines and red wine in the bar.
I didn't spill a drop but fevered as I slept,
my newly-dyed hair inking lilac onto the sheets.
All night it was the gales, not the docks' rumble

that rolled me over, or would have, if it wasn't
for the wrenched muscle. The next morning
was a pulled pint full of light, and the sea flicked
up the white undersides of its leaves. I'd got away
scot-free, was on the long run from several angles.

Or so I claimed. Too soon: watch me, full of glitzy
thoughts, tip half a carton of Co-op milk
into my borrowed rucksack, pour out half an hour
scrubbing with shampoo and the hotel towel,
only to mis-time the ebb tide of the first bus out.

One of the Summer People

It's hard to believe I am mere foreground flicker
in this place of deep time. This morning the new leaves

glowed like plum jam on the copper beech. I drew them
all afternoon; to you they're opaque and dropping now.

Ice bites the lake margins and falls back. Swans hatch, die.
No instrument is tuned to an interval of less than a decade.

Swimming, I barely trouble the meniscus, the islands
lie far beyond my stroke. In this timescale, trees rush up,

fresh and swift as grass. It's as if I see nothing alive –
oaks seem close to rock, stock-still columns of lignin;

you'd notice glass making its slow travel to thicken
the foot of the pane. It's no pretence: I'm blurred.

By the fells' long exposures I pass unrecorded. Always
someone in the damp cottage, but only the tang

of whippet holds, and the ink stain on the green curtain.
Between blinks I might be untenanted, whirled elsewhere.

See how I cook my baked potatoes in the microwave!
I'm seasonal trade. No one believes I've waited out my life

in other places. Even the bus drivers fail to notice me –
that shiver in the stop's air – on their heavy churn past.

Dove Cottage Ferns

By July they've bulked to a galleon's
massed rig of sail. Shrub-
broad, they're bold as gunnera

but feather-cut. From spring's
straight-up vectors, they loosen
and splay. I count out summer:

arc, arabesque, parabola, catenary –
a green apprenticeship of curve.
Impossible to chart the frill-edged

negative space under the clump's
awning, so sub-divided, it's a test
of fractal complexity for the nib.

Flip to the frond's reverse:
the future dried on like a code of dust.
Paired brown spore-cases mimic

infestation, but no: it's just life
holding the fort, biding its moment
to sprint and scatter. Crouched

behind a swag of Solomon's Seal,
I read a fern's microfiche, propagation
an abacus clicking away at my ear.

Was This Review Helpful to You?

There was a goat outside the window of my *Classic Double*,
working a bald strip of tilted earth behind wire.
Between us lay a five-foot-deep concrete alley
through glass; my admiration at its brown head and neck
on a white body, like two beasts severed and sewn;
and some prison dreams neither of us would divulge.

In the bar, low sun glimmed off the sea. I couldn't
get a seat near it. The men from the power station who could,
as a squadron, turned their heads from the window
to watch the TV above mine. For me too, it was hard
to believe in the beach that stretched for miles each side
like an adhesive strip ripped off something useful.

Breakfast was an open bag of Kingsmill White,
some soft croissants pouched in cellophane, plus
one bruised pear which I took out of fellow feeling.
I had to get us out of here: away from the owners
talking business in their sagging tracksuits, away
from this disowned ground, its hand-hot rain.

Poem in the Voice of a Dead Cockroach

I, a mercenary from some other army
than the one into which you were bred,
suffered no conscription or signing up.

The egg, and the blood, made me a stalwart
for this trench, for trying to keep the pass open,
or (the same, the same – all wars being one)

trying to close the other pass, to oust
the bastard others out. In the guest bathroom
of a Spanish-style villa at Chung Hom Kok,

you'll find me: backflipped; dead afloat
in my long-boat carapace, six legs plaited
into caramel at the thorax. Failed antennae,

now slack as a ship's wake, pick up sod-all.
I am no Viking hero, just a beast born to this –
one whose team will outlast your lads

in the longest haul, albeit that tonight, you
or your poisons, Asian Pest Control,
have beaten my resolute, creaky body to it.

The Post Box in the Wall

She'd been there eight months when she saw it:
red-glossed, built into the slate car-park wall.
By then there was so much she needed to exile,
it was like absolution, its upper lip sheltering
inked addresses from the West Coast rain.

Often she lay in the cottage till nightfall,
whole days held under house arrest.
Her anger was rising like bread, full of air
that blew nobody good, the tar-tainted
breath of a chemical plant as it burned.

I won't even name the things she slipped
into that mouth, stumbling on cobbles
greased by the storms. Soon it wasn't enough;
she'd crouch by its cold scarlet vent, unhooded,
her hair carving wet lines down her face.

She'd talk like someone in court, spitting out rain
or whisper the snakes off her tongue. It's years:
no one lives there now. But to be frank, yes –
everything fed into the slot – the curses
and slurs – arrived, warm to the touch.

Prescription for a Middle-Aged Reader

Take one contact lens for the long view, one
for the fine print and the needle's slim traverse.

Yes, it works, after a fashion. I tilt my head
to the right as I read — until that eye is dense

with words — and nod out to the left. Which is
a sailor's eye, sea-scanning the bowl of hills

round Wirksworth, the dwarfish trees on the rise
where they buried the undertaker's horses.

On the moor, the reading eye falls back in its socket,
and I catch blades of fescue in high resolution.

Both I and the optician know, from following
the red light, that the distance eye is full of dead ground,

would hole sentences to knot-work and half-mist.
Let sky and grass and rocks close over the places

where the left eye looks, fritters away what it sees.

On a Woodblock Prepared for Engraving

Only one man in England makes these blocks
from frost-hard Christmas woods: holly
and box; pear – and fruitless lemonwood.
That one man sands the surface of the endgrain
to an almost oily smoothness, like something lifted
from a body, the silkiness of polished bone.

She touches the not-perfect rectangle.
Why use a resin blank when you can press
a single point into the matter of England –
its murky Christmasses, the tapers of dipped rush
heckling with spits of tallow, iron gutters
that fray rain from their blocked channels?

Finger and thumb steady the skew-cornered blank.
She always thinks of this as drawing,
burying light in the wood's claustrophobic density,
each stroke made over and over to avoid gouge.
At last, she will uncover it: the whole farm
needled into monochrome, two inches across.

Shocked into smallness, by days shrunk down
to fingerless gloves, she hoards the scrivening
of a single picture through several Christmasses.
Time spent in the studio on oil-heater afternoons
is spent in old money, easing the burin's beak
to build areas of white: the glaze between clouds,

lit stripes on a ploughed field. Sun pours
through the dead elms at the horizon
and scratches round the rooks' nests' spiky galls.
Let the puddings boil dry in their baby clothes.
Leave the tinsel coiled in snaky hibernation.
There is no need to invite anyone here.

Three Lessons in Ignition, 1 Sykeside

By morning the cinders have shivered
to dead-bird ash, fresh with the sting
and scent of phoenix. As I froth up dust
with the balding brush, I'm careful not to
share breath with the beast in the grate.

Once the blaze grips, it snickers and roars.
Is it legal to have this stuff alight in a house?
It gives off a pour of liquid gunmetal,
drugs up the room with visionary haze.
My jumpers reek of oil spill, firebomb.

The new coal shines like a horse's coat.
It's Chinese ink, with its furious black.
So full of muscle, this dense, sulky rock.
A coal-scuttle's a reflex waiting to kick:
a wrecked car poised on top of a cliff.

On the Last Evening We Watch Movies in Bed

This glass of water is a flat lake, and lightless too.
As I reach across the pillows, its curved shoreline

stretches, navy under black-green pines. It's calm:
not yet the brute flicker of the thriller's plot twist.

Hold my hand for this bit, comrade of my heart;
the Mexican bean pulse of your wrist betrays you

even in the dark. Mica chips in concrete reflect
nothing much. The killer walks across a car park,

his thin shoes on a matte stage. I can't smell him.
No one can: murderous brain chemistry spins off

less odorous jetsam than our bedsheet cache
of broken pheromones. You tell me to drink:

it's tasteless, scentless. When I put the glass down
the TV screen nearly loses itself in the shake.

It can't be you I'm afraid of, nor my face, drowned:
it's not knowing the name of the weapon he will bring.

I cannot doubt the end, the dazzling butchery
even I applaud. I nuzzle at your legionary's beard

as I wait, in a fever of guessing: his likely accessories,
what he hums, his cool, now irreversible, moves.

The Hostess

Marks of Possession by Demons: ... Also in the use of pronouns... the subject "possessed" is generally spoken of in the third person and regarded for the time being as in an unconscious state and practically non-existent.
— J L Nevius DD, *Demon Possession and Allied Themes* (1896)

'*My incense burner*' is how a demon may talk
of his host, the girl he found fetching water
by the path, her mind packed off elsewhere.
The demon is using her tongue, in comfort,
far from priests and their armoury of tricks
for ouster. '*My girl*,' says the demon, fondly.
Gladstone's book pointed out how they are
usually women, without education, and rural;
how possession so often comes upon us
off the beaten track. And now he is lying
in a hammock, wearing her skin, her breasts.
You may notice her beautiful nails are broken,
how she scratches the long muscles of her legs.
Other than that, the girl is the same,
but her substance is boiling off as a tribute
for the exacting demon — it drew him
and its fragrant burnout is keeping him home.
This is the moment she would have caught
sight of her husband-to-be, going to hunt
but she's muttering in languages known only
to adepts, turns away, nails harassing
her itch. She spits in the dust, an impossible
liquid: too dark for saliva, too light for blood.

The Piñata

No one told me to do it, but I was thorough
as a vigilante with the hammer. Blame it
on the hitman's ghost-written bio, cast aside
after thirty pages of full-on true-crime gore.

Some sliver must have cut me, his flick-knife
needling my brain to this ribbon of dream.
My boy was a looter, blond as a surfie, long-calved,
his stealings in a bin-bag gripped at the neck.

I didn't care if the whole street saw me breaking
his head, a smashed piñata of bone and blood.
I rocked him over and turned even the back
of his skull to pieces of jigsaw. You laughed –

remember? – when I told you next evening
as we lay smug as saints in our new linen sheets.
Half-stunned, you muttered some kindness:
a person can't swing for a crime in the brain.

Yet I noticed you moved to the bed's outer
edge as you slept; and I wasn't surprised when
I placed my palm on your back, to feel you
recoil as a snail might quiver at trial by salt.

The end was still months off, but I'd already
started to think about him: the hitman, who'd
called me with the lure of my out-of-character
sleep, whose encyclopaedic hands were full

of the worst kind of knowing. He could sleep
easy next to anyone mute. He'd hug me all night
in arms as steady as blockboard, wise enough
to his way with his fists to give dreams a miss.

Temptation

When we turned the corner of our little shelter we saw the Church & the
whole vale. It is a blessed place. The Birds were about us on all sides –
Skobbys Robins Bullfinches.
     – Dorothy Wordsworth, *Grasmere Journal*, Friday 30th April 1802

In my dream the Devil led me to this church
and showed me Grasmere from above
like a frock cast off and wrinkled on the ground,
like a picnic rug set out with fresh-cut
brown bread sandwiches and pots of salmon mousse.

Go on, he said: *climb the roof slope to the ridge*
and hug the flagpole in the way you'd
only hold your lover. The lake was so –
well, so much like a mirror
that you couldn't even see that's what it was.

I was sold, and took the pint of misty yellow
scrumpy he passed up. The birds were all around us
but invisible, and from the trees like bright-green cumulus
each one was shrieking: *Don't!* I smiled and took a sip.
Ask if I signed the contract: I'll say nowt.

Songs from West Cumbria (5)

Room 204 (Double for single use)

This is the room of tongues,
their busy pink-on-pink textures:
rose plush, plum chintz, the tiles
in the bathroom as marbled
as their meat when spiced and tinned.

Look at the placement of mirrors:
the wall-sized gilt affair alongside
the pilastered bed, swallows
the room in its gold-lipped mouth
and returns it redder and less itself.

Most of all it is not from the bed
but beside the bed, that you note
someone has angled an oval glass
on the mahogany chest of drawers
so you see your pear-shape precisely

from the back as you climb
onto the high mattress. An unordinary
thing: that candid pink-satin-framed
rear view. Intimate for single use,
you claim this tanless, tapered skin.

All the kittens' rough tongues
are talking at once under the black beams
like a ship creaking its timbers
as you dip and swim in the watery
fetch between mirror and mirror.

The Madonna of Oxfam

The tangerine dress comes with its own breasts —
higher and bigger and closer together than mine.
I'm not ungrateful: I'll borrow their secondhand air
in stiffened cones let into the bodice lining. I like
the hand-embroidered label, the trouble she took,
the specialness cotton dresses once used to have.
Fifty years on, the material still feels live, unpapery,
not just an exhibit of how she lived. For the rest,
the Le Creuset-coloured frock fits like a dream —
not, as things do now, with Lycra's eager adjustments.
It's someone's just-married summer again, as soon
as the splashy pattern lays itself out in pleasure
on my bones. It comes to mind how the English
took to imported cotton; people said silk underwear
never felt clean. You think you know what's what
on days like these, then some other woman steps out
from behind the curtain for trying-things-on,
more than dressed-up, a great deal less than decent.

The Knowledge

Eyes shut to the white morning, it's all yours:
the scarlet glory under your eyelids' canopy.

You could ask your husband to turn them inside out,
as the optician does, checking for lesions. He'd read

nothing but a delta he has no need to navigate.
The dentist lifts your tongue in a square of gauze.

All day in the stockroom that jumpy muscle plays
along the scratched inner surfaces of your teeth.

Whoever traced that coast has since moved on.
What lasts is the show that's put on just for you:

a private voice strained through your deck of bones.
No one hears you speak with quite that note

about the friction of your arteries in flood, tales
from the place where all your skins are soft-side in.

You don't ask how it is for him. You're just a couple
who walk back each week from the bar, hands curved

in the memory of pints. If there's a lesson, you learn it
in sleep, by his breath on your sunburnt arm.

Exit, Through the Museum Shop

I pick up *The Hand Boiler* for something to do.
On the box is a picture in dayglo colours:
a mazy weave of glass-piped macramé, or
a helix of tubes flowing with fluorescent liquid
looped back on themselves and sealed. What sits
in that bulb of glass is no comfortable fluid,
its name a warning in Latin. I flip up the lid;
the thing is coddled in bubble wrap. So fragile,
maybe best to leave it and its cargo alone.
I can imagine: the globe will rest in the palm,
its volatile pool of purple, cyan or lime quiescent
for now. Just body heat will set it to bubble
and spit, some unearthly moisture doing its nut.
I'm calm. I keep my palms gloved, heart
as muffled as my hands. Perhaps even now
in its box, the Hand Boiler's blistering cocktail
is churning away as if the world had just started
to cook into soup. I'd have said that what I felt
for you once is now tepid, tinged with contempt.
But out here in deep space even that modest heat
drives this stuff to punishing point, to the mark
on the scale where I wanted to be all along:
to simmer, to hard boil, to absolute cauldron.

The Corner Shop

Neighbours thought it was
gunfire, but inside the boys
were throwing bottles around.

When the snow was bad,
he brought milk and bread
to his regulars on a sledge.

The brain in which he gathered
memories to feast on in old
age (when the skin's pickings

are thinner), the life spent
holding that vessel carefully
as heavy water, the boys

cracked with a claw-hammer.
The stock-take of
birth and death – it was all

flowing. They were still in there,
swimming, shouting, when
the first witnesses arrived,

to snag at the locks. No one
on that street had ever seen
red like this, or so much weather.

Elterwater Rain

When I came to write of it there was no rain,
just the last of its ectoplasm shivering
in a pool on the terrace's lowest slate.

No sky winks in the left-behind liquid,
only the garden table's black metal underside –
all is prediction, absence, an oracle's glum vigil –

whilst the air, hyperactive, holds more weather:
weather folded in weather, the rest of the day
remains to be dealt like a deck of wet cards.

Town rain splits and skids but this land accepts
what is given. Foliage moves against foliage;
water drains down the conifers' inner ladders.

Something thirsts for each substance spilled
but this liquid is neighbourly, a local's drink.
Outside Ambleside's tourist shops, dog-bowls

brim with downpour. Here the last shower
hangs about too, old drops slung like bats
from the bird-feeder and the patio chairs.

The Evacuees

Free is kissing the accelerator, gently at first,
then rattling the hired van down Cattle Drift
out of the too-close breath of the river lane,
past the sewage farm and the pebbled church.

The hollow rear doors of the van hold back
my blossoming duvet but some chimney-
trapped bird in my chest lifts off, only singed.
I haven't known happiness like it for a year.

We scarpered a day early, with the modesty
of minor crims, truants pinching ourselves.
Everything is copper under each street lamp's
rain-stripes and we drop a letter at the pub.

In an hour we're just north of Manchester
in the tunnel of a short-run snowstorm,
clots of slush spattering the van. My brother's
talk is so fresh it's just come on the market.

A vehicle this loaded makes for trouble on the road.
We're that careful with our hunger we don't
stop for coffee, a sandwich, a piss. Until
we're home, nothing enters, nothing leaves.

Antidote

... the banging of windows and the crashing of glass are the robust sounds of fresh life, the cries of something new-born.

– Elias Canetti

The fallen-forward mirror shows its brown-paper back
and picture wire, a coffin to the alp shapes of its smash.

That hieroglyph is her next seven years lying there,
spoiled to vinegar before they were even toasted in.

The day drops onto the shattery smile. Spring sinks
below six degrees, and new grass chokes on its growth.

The antique shop man tells her: take two shards and break
again. She slaps glass twice on the yard's old quarries.

The noise is as sharp as the jets that pierce the valley,
stitching their nose cones through bled air. Too easy

for a shake in the wrong hands to spend all the luck
she had leaned on to get here. It's time to trust to charm,

that a double blow back will unravel seven years of sour tides.

Memorial

Your photos are the thing that remains
where our hands lock in prisonish happiness

like dogs disturbed at mating, who stuck.
These days there's no need for bonfires,

for cellophane quilling off the print, or smuts
on next door's pegged-out pale wash.

All this is a history I learned from the old,
who would stir like hounds at something to hide.

Trackless and snug in the study, I drill down
and discard, but my brain still holds you afloat

on its slow meniscus, like cumulonimbus
copied from sky onto the ocean's calm plate.

The noises you and I made are certainly lost.
My mouth tries them out and can't find the shape.

Deep in the archives, the music-hall blood
that did all this to us is still hot, but it's clotting

to a substance as glossy and brittle as marble,
into which an inscription could be carved.

Coal

If you can call it that, the coalman comes
with smokeless: tidy nuggets in quarter-tonne bags;
that unbalanceable, barely incendiary fuel.
But it's heavy still and I see him wince
as he hauls the sacks down the wet slate steps.

Sometimes luck comes in with it, glad-handed
by a dark-haired man at the turn of the year.
Bede wrote that coal smoke scattered serpents.
The real thing sings like a cake not yet cooked,
but this just whispers to itself in the grate.

He must be cold and he tells me his daughter
has seen two husbands die. Illnesses borrow
their names from coal's heat and singe.
Even after it's burned it's bad: sweeps died
from the soot grained into their skins in the climb.

So I wish the coalman – and his daughter –
luck, in our casual chat. May that chancy rock
earn him a long retirement: vertebrae sound
and separate; money enough to buy him warmth.
May adders slither from the path at his tread.

King Tak Hong Porcelain,
Queen's Road East, Wan Chai

I wanted the pottery pumpkin, ten-lobed
        in yellow, red and green.
I wanted to sit at home on the barrel stool
        with its wraparound blue mountains.
I would have wanted the dragon cake-stand
        if it hadn't had a gold edge.

I needed dishes for earrings and soy sauce,
        half-a-dozen lids to hold my tea's heat.
I wanted the soap-green plastic coat-hangers
        with the swivel hook, plus pencil pots
brushed with wrist-flicky crustaceans, waving
        their one-stroke feelers under glaze.

I wanted fifteen years of my life back,
        to start here again: bone-china-skinned
and mouthy, a bleached flag of sweat drawing down
        the neon blaze of the Cup Noodle Building
onto my skinny chest. I wanted the slowed replay,
        to share it with you once over.

My wish list: our first date in the hardware shop
        (I've kept both of the green mugs
now full of sensitive toothbrushes and floss);
        some other things I've thought better of since;
most of all that night-long bare-faced seduction
        under the cool eyes of your tropical fish.

We Prayed for a Man Without a Beard

*My Tooth broke today. They will soon be gone. Let that pass I shall be
beloved—I want no more*
   – Dorothy Wordsworth, *Grasmere Journal*, Monday 31st June 1802

As the hygienist scrimshaws round my gum
I stretch my small mouth wide as horror.
She learned on a metal skull with white teeth
painted with a black stain to be scraped clean.

When she grew exact, they covered the head
with a rubber sheath – lipped, eared, with hair –
which hugged the mouth's airy cathedral,
its cloisters filled with the breath of winter.

For months a hand scaler was all she held.
In the exams they were tested on people:
*We prayed for a person with a big mouth
and small teeth; we prayed for a man without a beard.*

I feel my face grow tight, and sickening
as a mask on my skull's frame. After death
rot will strip it down to show the teeth I held,
coddled by the hygienist's intricate decades.

Then the cool breezes off the fells will blow
over the roots. My phantom head smiles:
free at last of the pornography of skin.
I pray for a man to kiss me, while I live.

Sweet Sixteen by a Cold Wall

Cross as two sticks, I lie in the folded sheets of my last bed,
stuck in cold storage. The soft planes of my puppy-fat face
slope in bisque marble, matte as old bread.

Only my bare foot shines where the church tourists always
rub. Their held breath hums like a loaded drinks-chiller.
Nothing but set rock travels my limed arteries,

and all I want is to live again, like a real girl: to hold
down a telesales job, to sweet-talk punters with standard
greetings, and marry too young; to stand at the altar

up the duff in stretch lace, bring up child after child,
giving the finger to time with every hard breech
birth; to be warm flesh today, ungoverned and dicey as yeast.

Songs from West Cumbria (7)

It Is Harder to Leave Sand than to Be Left by Sand

For a while in Arnside I became a student of sand.
It was mischance. My first degree was not in sand.
The first day I laboured at its mutable alphabet

from the Parker Knoll chair in my second-floor room.
My eyes were mere instruments: to measure glitter
in the pyrotechnics of sand, the speed of the tide's sprint.

At first I did not touch sand: I extracted no cores
from the sea-stripped estuary, nor tried with fine tweezers
to pick the lock of a sand as varied as coloured tweed.

The second day I trod the shore like a seamstress,
folding yards of sand across my body. Its skirt lengths
rolled from the viaduct to the Promenade, frayed there.

I stitched a grass-fine dress in which to marry sand.
I made a mood board for my sky-blown wedding:
chose the bisque's dust, the slurry drag of slaked sand.

On the third day I left, after a light breakfast: ringless,
sceptic, unaltered by my visit. My suitcase was empty;
I carried with me: the cuff of the wind, skiffs, sand.

Praise Poem for the Urbanites

Too soon I felt the loss of the city. The pull
of its mass – all of you clustered there – held me.
I was drawn out of true by the physical drag

of what I have to call *longing,* here in the open:
a countryside plugged with delicate stony towns,
hamlets kept apart by nothing but space.

Where you are, lights twitch in the air.
An unnatural fur clings to the back of the fridge.
Your balconies leave me no room to run

but from the church green, where I hang
under the sound of bells, I can feel you all stir –
oh my cellmates! – in a proximate sleep I've never left.

I take a stroll at dawn to the flooded quarry.
The whole sodding time I think of you dancing,
electrics fizzing in your brains a handspan apart.

I'd take it back: life as a farmed salmon, oily
with antibiotics and omega 3, abraded fins
wafting in over-cooked water. Or, the press

of bodies in our tankful of harvestable muscle.
I want this: the shift of skin's anonymous touch,
the warmth on the other side of the wall.

Acknowledgements

Thank you to the editors of the following publications where some of these poems were published: *Hallelujah for 50ft Women: Poems About Women's Relationship to their Bodies*, edited by Raving Beauties (Bloodaxe, 2015), *Kenyon Review Online* (www.kenyonreview.org), *The London Magazine, Mslexia, New Statesman, New Welsh Review, The North, Oxford Poetry, Poems In Which* (www.poemsinwhich.com), *Poetry Ireland Review, Poetry London, The Poetry Review, Smiths Knoll, Sounds of the Front Bell* (The Group in association with Stonewood Press, 2014), *The Spectator, Wordsworth Trust Messenger*.

'This Is Not a Garden' won 1st prize in the Kent & Sussex Open Poetry Competition 2013 and 'King Tak Hong Porcelain, Queen's Road East, Wan Chai' won 1st prize in the 2013 Café Writers' Competition.

Several of the poems appeared in *One of the Summer People* (Wordsworth Trust, 2013), a pamphlet of work from a year as Poet-in-Residence at the Wordsworth Trust in 2013. Considerable thanks go to the Trust for its generous hospitality, and to the Arts Council for funding the residency.

I am very grateful to Gladstone's Library where I was Writer-in-Residence in June 2014. Many thanks for the gift of time and a precious space in which to work, and to Peter Francis, Louisa Yates and everyone else at Gladstone's for their kindness.

Many thanks for the support of Arts Council England in the form of a grant in 2014 which enabled me to complete this book.

Special thanks go to Nigel, my parents & Loretto, Joanna & Richard & Soshan (for the two-way visits and a lot more), Katrina (for much collaboration and comment as well as friendship), Lindsay, Ian, Ed, Chrissie, Tim, Anne, Wanda, John and the Group, Richard (for the books) and Amy Wack and the team at Seren.

All quotations from Elias Canetti are from *Crowds and Power* (The Seabury Press, New York, 1978), translated from the German by Carol Stewart.

Well chosen words

Seren is an independent publisher with a wide-ranging list which includes poetry, fiction, biography, art, translation, criticism and history. Many of our books and authors have been on longlists and shortlists for – or won – major literary prizes, among them the Costa Award, the Jerwood Fiction Uncovered Prize, the Man Booker, the Desmond Elliott Prize, The Writers' Guild Award, Forward Prize and TS Eliot Prize.

At the heart of our list is a good story told well or an idea or history presented interestingly or provocatively. We're international in authorship and readership though our roots are here in Wales (Seren means Star in Welsh), where we prove that writers from a small country with an intricate culture have a worldwide relevance.

Our aim is to publish work of the highest literary and artistic merit that also succeeds commercially in a competitive, fast changing environment. You can help us achieve this goal by reading more of our books – available from all good bookshops and increasingly as e-books. You can also buy them at 20% discount from our website, and get monthly updates about forthcoming titles, readings, launches and other news about Seren and the authors we publish.

www.serenbooks.com